A TASTE OF MEXICO

Linda Illsley

Thomson Learning

New York

Titles in this series

A TASTE OF

Britain	Italy
The Caribbean	Japan
China	Mexico
France	Spain
India	West Africa

Cover *A pyramid temple built by native Mexican people long before the arrival of the Spanish.*

Title page *The floating gardens near Mexico City.*

First published in the
United States in 1995 by
Thomson Learning
115 Fifth Avenue
New York, NY 10003

First published in Great Britain in 1994 by
Wayland (Publishers) Ltd.

Library of Congress Cataloging-in-Publication Data
Illsley, Linda
A taste of Mexico / Linda Illsley
p.   cm.—(Food around the world)
Includes bibliographical references and index.
ISBN 1-56847-186-6
1. Cookery, Mexican—Juvenile literature.
2. Food habits—Mexico—Juvenile literature.
3. Mexico—Social life and customs—Juvenile literature.
[1. Cookery, Mexican. 2. Food habits—Mexico.
3. Mexico—Social life and customs.] I. Title. II. Series.
TX716.M4I43   1994
641.5972—dc20   94-27120

Printed in Italy

Contents

Mexico and its people

The land and climate

Mexico is in the southern part of the North American continent. To the north it borders the United States, and to the south it borders the Central American countries of Guatemala and Belize. To the west of Mexico is the Pacific Ocean; to the east is the Gulf of Mexico. Mexico is the fifth largest country in the American continents, after Canada, the United States, Brazil, and Argentina.

The coastlines of Mexico are tropical and warm; coconut palms grow easily there.

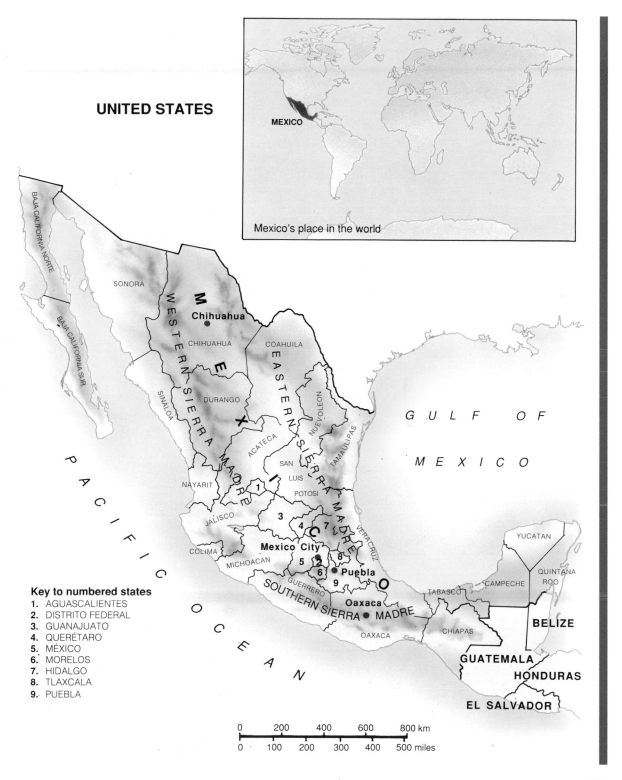

UNITED STATES

MEXICO

Mexico's place in the world

BAJA CALIFORNIA NORTE

BAJA CALIFORNIA SUR

SONORA

WESTERN SIERRA MADRE

M
Chihuahua

CHIHUAHUA

COAHUILA

EASTERN SIERRA MADRE

E

X

SINALOA

DURANGO

NUEVO LEON

ACATECA

NAYARIT

SAN LUIS POTOSI

TAMAULIPAS

I

GULF OF MEXICO

1

3

JALISCO

4   **C**   7

Mexico City

COLIMA

MICHOACAN

5   **2**

8

VERACRUZ

6   ● **Puebla**

9

GUERRERO

O

YUCATAN

QUINTANA ROO

CAMPECHE

TABASCO

Oaxaca

SOUTHERN SIERRA MADRE

BELIZE

OAXACA

CHIAPAS

GUATEMALA

HONDURAS

EL SALVADOR

Key to numbered states
1. AGUASCALIENTES
2. DISTRITO FEDERAL
3. GUANAJUATO
4. QUERÉTARO
5. MÉXICO
6. MORELOS
7. HIDALGO
8. TLAXCALA
9. PUEBLA

PACIFIC OCEAN

| 0 | 200 | 400 | 600 | 800 km |
| 0 | 100 | 200 | 300 | 400 | 500 miles |

A taste of Mexico

Above *Some of Mexico's old volcanoes are so high they are covered with snow. This volcanic mountain is outside Mexico City.*

Mexico has almost every type of climate. It has hot deserts, humid rain forests, cold mountainous regions, and warm coastal areas. With such a range of climates, Mexico produces a wide variety of food, including three of its main crops – corn, wheat, and rice.

The state of Oaxaca (pronounced wha-hack-a) has many mountains and is very dry. Look for Oaxaca on the map on page 5.

The people

Mexico has a population of over 92 million. More than two-thirds of these people live in cities and small towns; the rest live in rural areas. Mexico City, the capital of the country, has more than 20 million people. It is the second most populated city in the world.

Most Mexicans would describe themselves as *mestizos*. A *mestizo* is someone who is a descendant of both native Mexicans (called Indians) and

Mexico City is in a valley.

Southern Mexico is covered with rain forests.

Europeans. The Indian peoples were the first to live in what is now Mexico. In 1519, the first Europeans – the Spanish conquerors – arrived. The Spanish gained control over the region, and Mexico was ruled by Spain until 1821.

Today, Spanish is the language that most Mexicans speak. However, there are about five million Mexicans who live in communities where more than 50 Indian languages are still spoken. These communities keep alive many ancient Indian traditions, including some very special ways of cooking.

Above The Spanish conquerors enslaved the native Mexicans, as illustrated by this mosaic wall by Mexican artist Diego Rivera (1886–1957).

Right These children, who live in the rain forests in the south, follow many of the traditions of their Indian ancestors.

The history of Mexican food

Before the Spanish arrived

Before the Spanish arrived in Mexico in 1519, the Indians had a very efficient system for producing food to feed the population, which was then about 30 million people.

Among the most interesting ways of producing food was the *chinampa,* which was a floating island in a shallow lake. The Indians made a *chinampa* by piling up plants and mud until there was a surface on which crops could be grown. *Chinampas* were very fertile, producing up to three harvests in one year, and the plants grown on them never needed watering. Nowadays, the only *chinampas* left are in a park near Mexico City, which is shown on the title page.

Indians also used to grow a wide variety of fruits, vegetables, and medicinal

This mural, also by Diego Rivera, shows chinampas *(in the background) and how they were cultivated by the Indians.*

A taste of Mexico

There were many great civilizations in Mexico before the Spanish arrived. Scientists are still trying to discover all the mysteries surrounding the ruins of those civilizations.

plants in courtyards behind their houses. Some courtyards had as many as one hundred different plants, so they were an important source of food. Today, people in small villages in the Yucatan region of southeastern Mexico still have courtyards, but courtyards have disappeared from the cities.

The courtyard of this Mayan family has papaya trees, watermelons, and flowers.

This market has many types of fruit for sale.

When the Spanish arrived, they were amazed at the assortment of foods in the marketplaces. There were great varieties of fish, seafood, meat from wild animals, corn, fruits, and vegetables. The Indians carried all these foods to the markets on foot. There was no other form of land transportation until the Spanish brought oxen, horses, and donkeys to Mexico.

Salt and cacao beans, from which chocolate is made, were important for Indian societies because they were used as money as well as food.

A taste of Mexico

Although plowing is done with tractors all over the country, in some areas you can still find people using oxen or horses to pull a plow.

The exchange of foods between Mexico and Europe

The Spanish traveled to Mexico in large ships, and they carried with them many things that were new to that part of the world. These included foods such as wheat, onions, rice, oranges, apples, and sugarcane, which were soon being grown all over Mexico. The Spanish also brought farm animals such as oxen, cows, pigs, sheep, goats, and chickens, and their own farming tools such as the plow and the hoe, which became part of the Mexican system of food production.

On their trips back to Europe, the Spanish took with them foods from Mexico, such as corn, potatoes, tomatoes, and cacao beans, that were new to Europeans. Gradually, these new foods became an important part of the European diet.

In Yucatan, the soil is very rocky. This man is planting corn with a digging stick, the way the Maya did before the Spanish arrived.

Mexican dishes

There is a great variety of Mexican dishes, which is not surprising in a country with so many different climates and foods and with the influences of both Indian and Spanish cooking traditions. Each region has its own special dishes that are made nowhere else. For example, anise leaf and corn soup is a speciality in the state of Michoacan. Other dishes, such as tacos and tortillas, are made all over the country and are becoming well known outside Mexico.

Taquitos made with corn tortillas can be filled with almost any food, such as potatoes, beans, or meat. Taquitos are rolled up and fried. The wooden bowl at the side contains guacamole, a salsa made from avacados, to be served with the taquitos.

Mealtimes

Above *Tortillas are used in Mexico very much like bread is in other countries.*

Mexican dishes usually take a long time to prepare because they use mostly fresh ingredients. In the past, people shopped every day in the local market; today, people in the cities shop less frequently and often go to supermarkets instead.

Most Mexicans have tortillas, a kind of pancake made from ground corn, with every meal. Breakfast for people in the cities may include packaged cereals such as cornflakes, fruit, eggs with tortillas and beans, or some sweet bread. For people in villages, breakfast may be tortillas, beans, meat in a hot sauce, or *posol* (a drink made with ground corn, water, and salt, with chili or honey added). Workers in the fields often have a mid-morning snack of *posol* or tacos, which are filled tortillas.

Lunch, between one and three o'clock in the afternoon,

These children are mixing their posol *with water to make a nutritious snack.*

14

is the main meal. People used to have a few hours off from work to go home and eat, but in the cities this is changing. Lunch might include chicken or vegetable soup, rice or pasta, a meat casserole, vegetables, beans, tortillas or bread, a fresh fruit drink, and dessert.

The evening meal is normally light, and there is no fixed time for it. It may be just a cup of hot chocolate and sweet bread or a couple of quesadillas, which are tortillas with melted cheese in them.

Mexicans like to have snacks made from regional dishes, and the many street sellers offer these foods. There are also special taco restaurants; the good ones are always full, and people travel long distances to eat there.

This street seller is offering all kinds of ready-to-eat fruit – coconut, papaya, orange, mango, and jicama – that you can have with limes, salt, or powdered chili, as a snack.

Corn and wheat

Corn, also known as maize, has been the most important crop for Mexicans for thousands of years, and there are many legends about how people first came to eat this grain. According to one Aztec legend, Quetzalcoatl – an Aztec god – turned himself into a red ant and stole the sacred corn seeds from other gods. He brought the corn as a gift to the humans so they could feed themselves. Even today, in Indian villages, the first ears of corn that are harvested are offered to the god Quetzalcoatl to thank him for his gift.

Corn is grown all over Mexico.

Corn is a cereal that grows in almost all climates. Every part of the corn plant is used – as food, fuel, or medicine. Even the worms that eat the corn and the fungus that grows on it are considered special foods.

There are about 2,000 Mexican recipes for using corn. It is easy to cook with corn because it goes well with many other foods, such as beans or chilies. Corn is used dried or fresh, made into a main course, a soup, a dessert, or a drink. Most importantly, it is ground into flour and used to make tortillas.

In the past, tortillas were made in every house. If you walked down the

Above *Corn grains vary in color. When dry like this, they can be stored for a long time and used as seed or as food.*

Traditionally corn was ground by hand in metates *(see page 34) and the tortillas were then patted out by hand and cooked over a wood fire.*

street very early in the morning you would hear the gentle *pat-pat* sound of tortillas being made by hand. Today, tortillas are usually made by a machine, and it is quite common to see people lining up to buy fresh tortillas just before lunch. Handmade tortillas are now a treat for special occasions.

Once the corn is harvested, the stalks are dried and used as fodder for animals.

Wheat, which is grown in the north, is used to make all kinds of pastries, cakes, and sweet or savory breads. Bakers often work all night to make the next day's bread, so if you get to the bakery or the market early in the morning, the bread is still hot from the oven.

A specialty in the north is tortillas made with wheat flour. Wheat tortillas, which are whiter and much bigger than corn tortillas, are used in the same way as corn tortillas but in different dishes. The burrito, a wheat tortilla often filled with rice, beans, meat, and chili sauce, is very popular in the United States.

Wheat tortillas

Equipment

mixing bowl
dish towel
rolling pin
cast-iron griddle
   or heavy frying
     pan
spatula

Ingredients
Makes 12

1 cup all-purpose
   flour, sifted
4 tbl. butter
1 teaspoon salt
½ cup warm water
some extra flour

1   Put the flour in the bowl and rub the butter into the flour with your fingers.

A taste of Mexico

2 Dissolve the salt in the water and add it to the flour mixture.

3 Knead the dough well for about 5 minutes. Cover with a dish towel and set it aside for about 2 hours.

Always ask an adult to help you when working with a stove.

4 Heat the griddle or frying pan over low heat.

5 Knead the dough again for 2 minutes, then take a small piece of dough and make a ball about 1½ inches in diameter. Press the ball out on a floured surface and roll it into a circle about 7 inches across. It should be paper thin.

6 Place the tortilla carefully on the griddle (remember it is hot) and leave it for about 20 seconds. Turn the tortilla over with the spatula and cook the other side for about 15 seconds. You can eat tortillas right away or save them to be used later.

Quesadillas

1 Place the grater over a plate and grate the cheese. Divide the cheese into four equal portions.

A taste of Mexico

2 Heat the griddle or frying pan over medium heat. Place a tortilla on the griddle for about 5 seconds to make it soft. Use the spatula to put the tortilla onto a plate.

4 Place it back on the griddle and cook it until the cheese melts. Turn it over with the spatula a few times so that it does not burn, then put it on a plate.

Always ask an adult to help you when working with a stove.

3 Put one portion of the grated cheese inside the tortilla and fold it over.

5 Use the remaining tortillas and cheese to make three more quesadillas. Eat them after they have cooled down a little. Try them with a little salsa (see recipe on page 41).

Meat, fish, and other delicacies

Mexicans eat more beef and pork than any other type of meat. Far more beef is eaten in the north of the country, where there is plenty of grassland for cattle, than in the central or southern areas where grazing land is scarce. People in these areas eat pork, chicken, and turkey. Goat and mutton are popular for Sunday lunch, and they are often cooked in a spicy sauce.

Above *Meat is sold in markets. Pork crackling and spicy sausages called chorizo are a special treat.*

Left *Beef and goat meat are very popular in Mexico.*

23

A taste of Mexico

This family is selling live iguanas, which are used to make flavorful soups.

The seafood stall in the market is selling octopus and various types of shrimp.

Deer, snake, and iguana meat are eaten in places near the coasts. Some people believe that snake and iguana meat can be used to treat all kinds of illnesses.

In areas near the sea, people eat lots of fish and seafood. Fresh red snapper, one of the most popular fish, is often fried with garlic. Seafood such as conch, clams, and sea urchins are considered delicacies.

In the last few years, people have begun to farm carp, freshwater bass, and oysters, and they are becoming popular all over the country.

For hundreds of years, some insects, such as grasshoppers, have been part of the diet in the southwestern state of Oaxaca. Visitors to the market in Oaxaca City may be surprised to find piles of grilled grasshoppers, but if they try them, they may discover that grasshoppers are tasty.

Dairy products

The native people of Mexico learned how to make cheese from the Spanish. Cheese goes very well with corn and chili, so it was quickly adapted into Mexican cooking.

Today, there are many types of Mexican cheeses for sale in supermarkets or in local markets, where they can sometimes be bought from the people who made them.

Chihuahua cheese is made by German Mennonite communities outside Chihuahua City in northern Mexico. This cheese is slightly acidic and has a very creamy texture. It is used to stuff chilies or melt over food. *Adobera,* a slightly salty cheese, melts easily, which makes it ideal for quesadillas. *Anejo* cheese is aged and has a salty flavor and crumbly texture. It is perfect on many Mexican dishes such as tacos and refried beans.

Cheese is very popular and is used for many typical dishes.

Chilies and other spices

Chilies were first grown in Mexico, where there are around one hundred different varieties. Chilies vary in size, shape, color, and flavor. Each area has a type of chili that is grown locally and used in the cooking of that area. In the Yucatan region, people like to use the very fiery *habanero* chili in their sauces, whereas in the state of Sonora, they like a mild green chili.

Chilies can be used fresh or dried. Once dried, the flavor, color, and name of the chili changes, as well as its use. For example, the fresh green *poblano* chili is used to make stuffed chilies. Once it is dried, it is called *ancho* chili, is a deep reddish brown, and is used to make sauces such as the famous *mole* from Puebla (see page 37).

In most restaurants and at most family meals, at least one kind of salsa, or sauce, made with chilies is on the table. In Mexico, sauces are used to give food a

Far left *Chilies are used fresh, dried, or pickled. In the picture on page 26, you can see just a few of the different sizes, shapes, and colors of chilies.*

This one stall in the market is selling about thirty different kinds of chilies.

You have to take great care when cooking with chilies because they can irritate your skin, eyes, mouth, or any part of the body they touch.

Achiote seeds are bright red. In Mexico they are used as a seasoning for food, while in other countries they are used as a coloring.

more interesting flavor, just as salt and pepper are used in other countries. There are hundreds of sauces, and much of the time they are simply made with whatever ingredients are available.

Although chilies are very popular, not all Mexican cooking is hot and spicy. Many dishes, such as zucchini in a cream and cinnamon sauce, have very delicate flavors and are not hot at all. Mexican cooking uses lots of different herbs and spices. Fresh coriander, or cilantro, is a very popular herb for making sauces. There are about 13 different types of oregano used in the various regions, each claiming that their type is the most flavorful. *Epazote* is a strong herb, known in English as Mexican tea. It is used mostly in central and southern Mexico to flavor black beans and soups. It has a slightly musty flavor that takes some getting used to, but once people have had *epazote* a few times, they can develop a taste for it.

Achiote has a unique flavor. This small red seed from the *annato* tree is ground to a paste and mixed with other spices as a seasoning for meat and fish. A dish called *cochinita pibil* is made with suckling pig covered with *achiote* paste and the juice of bitter oranges, wrapped in banana leaves, and cooked in a pit in the ground for many hours. It is worth traveling to the Yucatan just to taste *cochinita pibil.*

Beans

Beans, like corn, are part of most Mexican meals. They go very well with meat, rice, and chilies. There are many ways of cooking beans, and almost every region has its own special bean dish. Most people agree that it is best to cook beans in a clay pot over a slow fire for a long time, sometimes up to three hours. Beans cooked this way are a favorite treat, especially with homemade tortillas and salsa.

There are many types of beans in Mexico. They come in all sizes and colors, such as the small black bean, the large white fava bean, and the pinto bean, which is a slightly purple bean with brown speckles.

Pinto beans are used to make Mexican refried beans. People often wonder why they have been fried twice. In fact, "refried" is a misleading translation of the Spanish word *refrito*, which means "thoroughly fried."

Some beans are sold dry in the market. There are many types to choose from depending on what dish they are going to be used for.

Other favorite foods

Vegetables and fruit

Tomatoes and onions are used in many Mexican dishes. They are often blended to make tomato sauce for eggs, pasta, rice, vegetables, or meat. Zucchini is a popular vegetable, and even the flowers are eaten fried or as a filling for tacos. In central Mexico, pumpkins, sweet potatoes, and plantains, a kind of banana, are cooked with brown sugar and served with milk for breakfast.

Zucchini flowers are cooked with onions and cheese and used as a filling for tacos, which is not only tasty but also pretty.

Above *Cooked cactus joints.*

Left *A nopal cactus plant with prickly pears.*

Below *Custard marrows can now be bought in some supermarkets in Europe and the U.S.*

Other very popular vegetables are nopal cactus joints, which are delicious when served as a salad mixed with tomatoes, coriander, and chilies, and custard marrow, which is good when baked in layers with egg and cheese.

If you ever visit a Mexican market, you might be surprised at the wide selection of fruits. There are many kinds of mangoes, papayas, and bananas. Besides the breakfast banana, there is a banana with a seed in it and another that is fried and served with savory food. Many fruits do not travel well, so they are not well known outside Mexico.

You can buy fresh-squeezed orange juice from street sellers in some Mexican cities.

Drinks

Because of the warm climate, cold drinks are an important part of the Mexican diet. In most cities, stores sell a wide variety of fresh fruit juices. Papaya-orange is a favorite. Sometimes fruits are blended with milk and cereals to make a more nutritious drink, which in other countries is called a smoothie (see recipe on page 39).

Some cold drinks are made with water, sugar, ice, and flavorings such as ground rice, hibiscus, or fruit. The supermarkets sell concentrates that are mixed with water, but they do not taste as good as homemade drinks. As in almost every country around the world, sugary soft drinks are very popular, especially served cold.

After a meal, people often have coffee. It may be instant coffee from the supermarket or freshly ground coffee from a local store. In some places, coffee is made in an earthenware pot and cinnamon is added.

Chocolate

Hot chocolate is said to have been the favorite drink of the Aztec king Montezuma. The word chocolate comes from the Aztec words *xoco,* meaning "bitter," and *atl,* meaning "water." The chocolate drink, or "bitter water," that the Aztecs drank was made with water, not milk, and it was not as sweet as the chocolate in candy, which has lots of sugar added. The Aztecs made chocolate by roasting the cacao beans and grinding them into a powder. They mixed the chocolate with perfumed flowers, honey, and vanilla and made it into different colors – red, white, orange, and even black.

The Spanish did not like chocolate at first. Eventually they got used to the flavor, and hot chocolate became a favorite drink.

Cacao beans grow in pods like the ones in this picture.

Cooking utensils

This woman is grinding corn in a metate. *She lives too far away from a city where she could buy it already ground.*

The most important cooking utensil for a long time was the *metate.* This is a sloping rectangular piece of volcanic rock, about 12 by 16 inches, with three legs. The *metate* is used to grind grains, especially corn, and chilies. The grains or chilies are placed on the *metate* and ground by pushing another long stone, also made from volcanic rock, against the *metate.*

In some small villages, people still grind food with the *metate,* but it is gradually being replaced by electric grinders and food processors.

The *molcajete* (pronounced moll-cah-hettay) is the Mexican version of a mortar. Also made of volcanic rock, it is bowl-shaped and has three short legs. The *molcajete* is used to grind spices and make sauces. Many people say that the best sauces are always the ones made in a *molcajete.*

Although many homes still have a *molcajete,* it is probably used only on special occasions, since most people in

Many people in the towns and cities have modern kitchens and now make their salsas using an electric blender instead of the traditional molcajete.

the cities have electric blenders or similar devices.

Today, many homes in the cities have stoves with ovens, and even microwave ovens. Yet in some places, cooking is still done on wood-fired stoves made out of clay. In the Mayan areas in the south, people still cook in pits in the ground called *pibs.* Cooking this way is very slow; sometimes it takes up to 12 hours for the food to be ready. But the results, such as *cochinita pibil,* are worth waiting for.

In some places, people still cook with wood. Many people claim that food cooked in this way tastes better than the food cooked on a gas or electric stove.

35

Festive foods

For some fiestas, children and adults dress up in traditional costumes similar to those worn by the Indians hundreds of years ago.

Food and music are always central to Mexican celebrations, or fiestas, and there are lots of celebrations in Mexico. Most Mexicans are Roman Catholics, so they celebrate all the major Catholic holy days. For each person there are at least two days to celebrate during the year – a birthday and, if he or she has been named after a saint, a saint's day.

Baptisms and weddings are big events. In the cities, a large hall and caterers are hired for the occasion. In the villages, all the women get together to start preparing the food two or three days before the party.

Perhaps the most popular festive dish is *mole,* which is made from about 28 different ingredients, including several kinds of dried chilies and a small amount of chocolate. The other ingredients may include almonds, tortillas, sesame seeds, chicken stock, onions, garlic, cloves, cinnamon, and bread. However, one of the traditions associated with *mole* is that each cook has his or her own recipe. *Mole* is usually served with chicken or turkey, rice, and beans.

Each region has certain dishes that are eaten on special occasions. In Mexico City people sometimes have stuffed chilies with a walnut and cream sauce, and in some states, such as Michoacan and Guerrero, they have a soup made with a type of dried corn called hominy, chilies, and three types of meat. Guacamole (an avocado dip), refried beans, and fried tortilla pieces are typical snacks during fiestas.

There are many other reasons for fiestas. Each region has different events to celebrate, depending on its local

Chilies with walnut and cream sauce. The red pomegranate seeds on top are used contrast with the green chilies and the white sauce. Red, green, and white are the colors of the Mexican flag.

A taste of Mexico

These sugar and chocolate skulls are made for the Day of the Dead. You can have a friend's name written on the strip on the forehead and give it as a present.

history. There are also national celebrations, such as Christmas, Easter, or the Day of the Dead (November 1 to 2) shared by everyone throughout Mexico.

The Day of the Dead has its roots in a mixture of Spanish and Indian cultures. It is not a sad day; it is a happy occasion when, according to belief, the souls of those who have died return to be with their families for a few hours. One of the preparations for the Day of the Dead is to make special kinds of bread and some of the foods that were the dead person's favorites when he or she was alive. The food is placed on an altar or taken to the cemetery and placed over the dead person's grave. The souls are believed to return to the world to share a meal with their families.

Roadside altars like this one often have food on them as an offering to the souls of those who have died.

Mexican smoothie

Equipment

electric blender or
    food processor
a glass

Ingredients
Serves 1

1 ripe banana
8 oz. milk
1 tablespoon
    honey
2 pinches ground
    cinnamon
3 drops vanilla
    extract

1   Put all the ingredients into the
blender or food processor.

2   Cover the pitcher and blend the
ingredients (except the cinnamon)
until smooth. Pour into a glass.
Sprinkle the cinnamon on top.

Make sure there is an
adult to help you
operate the blender or
food processor.

Salsa

Equipment

chopping board
knife
bowl
spoon

Ingredients
Serves 2 to 3

1 small onion or 6 to
   8 scallions
2 large, very ripe
   tomatoes
juice of 1 lime
salt to taste
a few coriander leaves

1   Chop the onion or scallions into small pieces.

Always ask an adult to help you when using a knife.

2   Put the chopped onion into the bowl and add the lime juice and a small amount of salt.

3   Wash the tomatoes and the coriander and chop them into small pieces. Add them to the bowl and mix with the spoon.

4   Allow the mixture to sit for five minutes, and then taste it to see if it needs more salt. Serve with quesadillas (see page 21), tacos, grilled meat or fish, or as a dip.

Guacamole

Equipment

chopping board
knife
bowl
spoon

Ingredients
Serves 2

1 large tomato
1 small onion
juice of 1 lime
salt to taste
1 large ripe
   avocado
a few coriander
   leaves

1 Wash the tomato and chop it into small pieces.

Always ask an adult
to help you when
using a knife.

2   Chop the onion fine.
Put it into the bowl with the
tomato. Add the lime juice
and some salt.

4   Wash and chop the
coriander. Add to the bowl
and mix everything with the
spoon. Taste and add salt if
needed.

3   Wash and peel the
avocado. Cut it into small
pieces and add to the bowl.

5   To keep the guacamole from
turning brown, keep the pit in
the bowl until ready to serve.
Guacamole makes a good dip at
a party. You could buy tortilla
chips or make tacos by filling
tortillas with guacamole. It is
delicious served as a side dish
with grilled meat or boiled rice.

Mexican fruit snack

Equipment

knife
chopping board
bowl
spoon

Ingredients
Serves 2

1 medium-sized
   cucumber
1 ripe mango
1 orange
1 papaya
half a pineapple
juice of 1 lime
salt to taste

1   Wash and carefully peel all the fruits.

2   Cut the fruit into bite-sized pieces and put into the bowl. Mix with the spoon.

3   Sprinkle with salt and add the lime juice. Mix everything together and taste to see if it needs more salt or lime.

Always ask an adult to help you when using a knife.

44

Glossary

Anise A small plant used to flavor food. The leaves and seeds, called aniseeds, taste like licorice.

Aztecs The people who ruled most of the central and southern part of present-day Mexico before they were conquered by the Spanish. The Aztecs had an advanced civilization with huge pyramids, temples, and palaces.

Baptism The ceremony used to admit a person, often a young baby, into the Christian church. Part of the ceremony involves pouring water over the person's head.

Capital The city from where a country is governed.

Caterers People who provide and serve food at gatherings and parties.

Cereal Any grain, such as wheat, corn, or rice, that is used for food.

Conquerors People who gain control, usually by force, over another group of people. The Spanish were conquerors of the native societies that lived in what is now Mexico.

Descendant A person who is the child or grandchild or great-grandchild, and so forth, of someone.

Diet The kind of food a person usually eats.

Dough A sticky paste made from flour and kneaded until it is elastic. Bread and wheat tortillas are made from dough.

Fertile When referring to soil, fertile means very rich and nourishing, thus helping plants to grow.

Grassland Land where grass is the main form of plant life.

Graze To feed on grass growing in fields.

Harvest The fruits, vegetables, or grains that are picked at the end of a growing season.

Hibiscus A plant with small red flowers that grows in sandy soil. The flowers are used to flavor drinks.

Hoe A tool with a long handle and a thin flat blade at the end, used for weeding and loosening the soil.

Hominy A whole, dried corn without the husk. It needs to be softened by boiling before it can be eaten.

Iguana A large lizard with a row of spines from its neck to its tail, found in warm climates of North, Central, and South America.

Indians The name the Europeans gave to the native peoples they found living in the Americas.

Knead To mix dough by folding over, pressing, and squeezing it by hand.

Legend A story that is handed down through the generations and believed to have some truth, although it cannot be proved.

Maya People who belong to the Indian peoples of the Yucatan area of Mexico. Before they were conquered by the Spanish, the Maya had a highly developed civilization with beautiful artwork and temples built on pyramids. Their knowledge of astronomy and mathematics was greater than that of any other culture at that time.

Medicinal Acting like medicine; able to cure illnesses.

Mennonite A member of the Mennonite Church, which was formed in Germany in the sixteenth century. Mennonites believe in plain, simple living. Today there are Mennonite farming communities in Europe and North America.

Mortar A very hard bowl in which substances are ground or pounded with a pestle. A pestle is a club-shaped tool, often made of stone.

Plow A tool used to break up and cut a groove in the soil so that it is ready for planting seeds.

Roman Catholics Members of the Roman Catholic Church, a Christian church headed by the Pope.

Rural Of the countryside.

Savory Having a salty or spicy taste; not sweet.

Tradition A custom or a way of doing something that has not changed for years.

Volcanic rock A fine-textured rock that forms when hot lava from a volcano cools down and hardens.

Books to read

Recipe Books

Coronado, Rosa. *Cooking The Mexican Way.* Easy Menu Ethnic Cookbooks. Minneapolis: Lerner Publications, 1982.

Gomez, Paolo. *Food in Mexico.* International Food Library. Vero Beach, FL: Rourke Publishing Group, 1989.

Wilkes, Angela. *My First Cookbook.* New York: Alfred A. Knopf Books for Young Readers, 1989.

Information Books

Howard, John. *Mexico.* Silver Burdett Countries. Morristown, NJ: Silver Burdett Press, 1992.

Lubeck, Maria-Garza and Salinas, Ana M. *Mexican Celebrations.* Austin: University of Texas at Austin, Institute of Latin American Studies, 1987.

Mayberry, Jodine. *Mexicans.* Recent American Immigrants. New York: Franklin Watts, 1990.

Pinchot, Jane. *The Mexicans in America.* Rev. ed. In America Books. Minneapolis: Lerner Publications, 1989.

Picture acknowledgments

The publishers would like to thank the following for allowing their photographs to be reproduced: Chapel Studios *cover* inset, 19, 21, 26, 39, 40, 42, 44; Greg Evans International *title page* (Miwako Ikeda), 8 top, (Miwako Ikeda); Eye Ubiquitous 32 (G. Howe); Catarina Illsley 10 bottom, 12 bottom, 14 bottom, 17 bottom, 28, 30, 31 top right; Life File 12 top (Caroline Field), 29 (Juliet Highet); Tony Morrison: South American Pictures 6 bottom, 7 top, 9, 11, 13, 14 top, 15, 16 (Robert Francis), 18, 23 both, 25 (Kimbell Morrison) 31 top left and bottom, 34, 35 top, 38 both (Robert Francis); Tony Stone Worldwide *cover*, 4 (Robert Frerck), 6 top (Robert Frerck), 7 bottom (David Hiser), 8 bottom (David Hiser), 10 top, 24 top (Ken Fisher), 36 (David Hiser); Wayland Picture Library 17 top (Skjold), 24 bottom (John Wright), 27, 33, 35 bottom (John Wright), 37 (John Wright).

The map artwork on page 5 was supplied by Peter Bull. The recipe artwork on pages 19 to 22 and 39 to 44 was supplied by Judy Stevens.

Index